Bilingual Edition

Let's Draw with Shapes™

Edición bilingüe

Let's Draw a
House with Shapes

Vamos a dibujar una
casa usando figuras

Joanne Randolph
Illustrations by Emily Muschinske

Traducción al español:
Mauricio Velázquez de León

The Rosen Publishing Group's
PowerStart Press™ & **Editorial Buenas Letras**™
New York

Published in 2005 by The Rosen Publishing Group, Inc.
29 East 21st Street, New York, NY 10010

First Edition

Book Design: Emily Muschinske

Photo Credits: p. 23 © Royalty-Free/CORBIS.

Library of Congress Cataloging-in-Publication Data

Randolph, Joanne.
Let's draw a house with shapes = Vamos a dibujar una casa usando figuras / Joanne Randolph ; illustrations by Emily Muschinske ; translated by Mauricio Velázquez de León.
    p. cm. — (Let's draw with shapes = Vamos a dibujar con figuras)
English and Spanish.
Includes index.
ISBN 1-4042-7558-4 (library binding)
1. Dwellings in art—Juvenile literature. 2. Drawing—Technique—Juvenile literature. I. Title: Vamos a dibujar una casa usando figuras. II. Muschinske, Emily. III. Title. IV. Let's draw with shapes.

NC1763.D85R36 2005
743'.84—dc22

                                          2004009674

Manufactured in the United States of America

Due to the changing nature of Internet links, PowerStart Press has developed an online list of Web sites related to the subject of this book. This site is updated regularly. Please use this link to access the list:
http://www.buenasletraslinks.com/ldwsh/casa

Contents

Contenido

Draw two big red rectangles to start your house.

Comienza tu casa dibujando dos rectángulos de color rojo.

5

Add an orange triangle for the roof of your house.

Agrega un triángulo anaranjado para dibujar el tejado de tu casa.

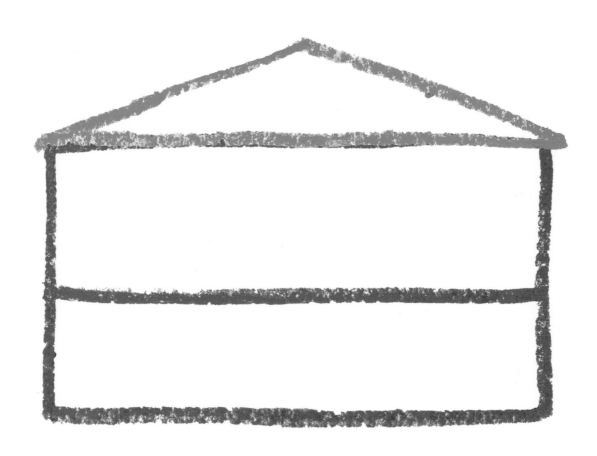

7

Draw two yellow squares
and one yellow rectangle
for some windows on
your house.

Dibuja dos cuadrados y un
rectángulo de color amarillo
para las ventanas de tu casa.

9

Add two green rectangles
for more windows on
your house.

Agrega dos rectángulos de
color verde para hacer dos
ventanas más en tu casa.

10

Draw a blue rectangle for the door of your house. Add one blue rectangle on each side of the door for posts.

Dibuja un rectángulo azul para hacer la puerta. Agrega un rectángulo azul a cada lado de la puerta para hacer las columnas de tu casa.

13

Add a purple triangle above the door of your house. This makes a small roof.

Agrega un triángulo de color violeta arriba de la puerta. Así dibujarás un pequeño tejado.

Add a pink triangle to the
main roof of your house.

Agrega un triángulo
de color rosa al tejado
principal de tu casa.

16

17

Add a black half circle to the pink triangle. This makes a new window on your house.

Agrega una ventana más a tu casa dibujando un semicírculo negro adentro del triángulo rosa del tejado.

Color in your house.

Colorea tu casa.

Many people live in houses.

Muchas personas viven en casas.

22

23

Words to Know/Palabras que debes saber

door/**puerta**

posts/**columnas**

roof/**tejado**

window/**ventana**

Colors/ Colores

 red/**rojo**

orange/**anaranjado**

 yellow/**amarillo**

 green/**verde**

 blue/**azul**

 purple/**violeta**

 pink/**rosa**

black/**negro**

Shapes/ Figuras

○ circle/**círculo**

▢ square/**cuadrado**

△ triangle/**triángulo**

▭ rectangle/**rectángulo**

⬭ oval/**óvalo**

⌓ half circle/**semicírculo**